introduced to him, they are going to remember Lee Stern...his voice, his smile, and his curiosity. In fact, he might be the most curious person whom I have ever met. He loves to ask questions, and he is a great listener.

As to him being mercurial, I would have to say that while he can be tough and challenging, I have been accused of being the same type of person. However, I think that the extra "gear" that Lee has, I also have, although I don't think I got it from him. I had it before I met him, but Lee honed it in me. But, all of the times that we had challenges when I was with the Sting, he helped me get through it. Sometimes it meant lighting a fire under me, but I sensed that he needed to do that and was doing it for a reason. I think that it was absolutely based on Lee's desire to seek and expect perfection. He is the ultimate perfectionist because he hates to lose and doesn't understand or accept losing, which is good and makes for a great leader. Simply put, Lee Stern holds himself and those around him to very high standards.

The tempestuous side of Lee would sometimes be demonstrated when I was with the Sting, including the times when I could hear his "conversations" with the team's coach Willy Roy, four offices down from mine, with all the doors closed. He probably thought that nobody could hear him, but the words being used in their "discussions" were quite clear to me and others in the office. Ironically, it gave me a greater appreciation for Lee's passion. He didn't and doesn't care if people know his true feelings and attitudes towards anyone, even though he is really a kind soul, as you will learn by reading his autobiography/biography.

Chapter One
Neighborhood Memories

If you are really interested in continuing, let's start from the beginning, according to the co-author of my autobiography!

It was two days after Christmas in 1926 at Michael Reese Hospital, located on Chicago's South Side,that became the first home of LEE B. STERN...THAT'S ME! At that time, my parents were living in an apartment on Juneway Terrace on the city's Far North Side in Rogers Park. I don't really remember my first three years of life, even though I was a BRILLIANT child...at least according to my parents.

I should note that my family's heritage is very important to me, especially the influences of my mom and dad, Natalie and Julie, best known as Tootsie and Jay. Mom grew up in a family with six siblings—four sisters and two brothers. Her father, Grandpa Shaloway, died when she was very young. The Shaloways had immigrated to America from Russia and settled in Cincinnati, but I was lucky enough to have fond memories of my Grandmother Shaloway, who died in April 1945 at the age of 84. Mother's siblings were all a bunch of characters. Among my aunts, Pearl was the only one who was single, and a top notch secretary. My Aunt Anna was a beautiful woman who was the oldest of my mother's brothers and sisters. She was married to Bob Higgins, the Irishman in the family. Then, there was my Aunt Rae, better known as "Re-Re," because she spoke French and had married my Uncle Jess, who retired at the age of 32 with a family fortune. He had been an attorney and, believe it or not, my aunt and uncle spent all of 1926 living in St. Tropez, France. Just think how far they were ahead of their time!

Then, there were my two very interesting uncles, Max and Julie, who were my mother's brothers and who specialized in handling the family's alcohol content. Mom's sister, Lillian, was the only one of the sisters who had children. Of course, her husband, Uncle Charlie, was an important part of that equation, too. Her children, cousins Elaine and Jerry, were both like a sister and brother to me.

Dad was born in Chicago, Illinois and lived his entire life on the Near North Side. He had a sister, Gert, who had one son, Allan. Dad's brother, Bernie, also had one son, Larry,

(L-R), My father's parents, Morris and
Rebecca Stern at their wedding, c. 1921; Norma's
father, Louis Retchin (born, 1897); Norma's mother,
Laura Retchin (born, 1901).

who tragically passed away from leukemia when he was only 29 years old, but left two wonderful sons, Brian and Ronnie. Dad's parents came to Chicago from Russia in the late 1890s and lived well into their late 80s.

My parents were married in 1924, and it is a rather interesting story how they met. Dad told me that he was walking down the street one day when a very young, good looking woman leaned out the window of the first floor of an apartment, where she was living with her mother, and threw a lasso around him. I heard that story for years. I don't know who really benefitted the most from that marriage, because they were divorced after twenty-plus years. But, thank goodness, they continued to have an excellent relationship.

Mom was born in Cincinnati Ohio, and Dad was born on Chicago's Near North Side. Grandpa Stern had a tailor shop on East Chicago Avenue, close to where Norma and I live today. For a while, Mom sold ladies' hats at a millinery shop at 2525 W. Devon Avenue in Rogers Park. Then, later, she went to work as the buyer and manager for the millinery department in the Fair Store, a major downtown Chicago department store. She became well known for customizing hats at prices that met everybody's budget.

As for my dad, he worked with my grandpa in what were called valet shops located in some of the hotels in downtown Chicago, but, unfortunately, they lost their business as a result of the Depression. The focus of the valet shops was to provide pressing, mending and cleaning services to hotel guests. So, when the business folded, Dad, who was really a natural salesman, got a job selling custom shirts, and, later, a position with Ross Federal Service, a theater checking agency. That job required Dad to travel all over the Midwest to cities that included Minneapolis, Detroit, and Indianapolis where he managed the RFS offices in those locations. My mom didn't want to travel with him and preferred to stay in Chicago with her excellent job, making sure that I spent most of my time doing the right thing...whatever that might be. Although it meant that my dad wasn't around during the week, he would be home on weekends, and, as far as I am concerned, it gave me the benefit of having love from both of my parents.

When Dad was working for Ross Federal, he also did some independent checking and was employed for a while by television icon "Uncle Miltie" Berle. Berle was a super guy, and, luckily, years later, I met him when Norma and I were on vacation at the famous Fontainebleu Hotel in Miami Beach, Florida. We were riding up in a hotel elevator when I realized that "Uncle Miltie" was standing near Norma and me. He turned to me and said, "What time do you have on the 'farkakte' watch you're wearing?" I was bold enough to say to him, "Hi, Mr. Berle, I'm Lee Stern and my dad, Jay, used to work for you in Chicago." His response was, "Was he a heavy-set guy?" I told him that was true. Berle said to me, "What a nice guy. How is he doing?" I had to tell him that my dad had passed away in 1953. A few years later, Berle was appearing at the Palmer House in downtown Chicago around the time of my mom's birthday. I went to the hotel to make a reservation for his show and learned that Berle was in rehearsals. I decided to say hello to him, and he remembered meeting me in Florida. When I told him that we were coming to the hotel to see his show because it was mom's birthday, he assured me that he would have the hotel seat us at a good table. He actually got us a location right in front of the stage and almost played his entire show to my mom, Tootsie. We were all thrilled by that experience!

My first school was Nettlehorst Elementary School at 3252 North Broadway where I remained until I completed third grade. It was an old, dilapidated school, built in 1892, and it probably was, and is, one of the oldest elementary schools still standing in Chicago. It was so overcrowded and deplorable that they had to use temporary structures to handle the additional students. Although I have the perception that the school should have been torn down years ago, it has now become a Magnet School and the first Chicago Public School Community School.

Among my earliest memories growing up was going to the Chicago Fire Department station on Chicago Avenue, just east of Michigan Avenue, behind the Water Tower. It has been there since the 1890s, and my dad, who grew up near that neighborhood, used to go there with my grandpa to observe the horse-drawn fire wagons. Since his father had taken him there, dad kept that tradition alive, and, years later, I repeated the same family tradition by showing my kids and my grandchildren that same fire station which is still functioning.

I really don't recall when I attended my first baseball game, but I do know that my Aunt Pearl tried to take me to the World Series in 1938 but couldn't get tickets for any of the games. Aunt Pearl also used to take me to wrestling matches and the roller derby at the Coliseum on South Wabash. I still remember the roller derby because those girls wore what seemed then like very short shorts while skating around the rink at high speeds, and, believe me, they were tough girls. Not only did Pearl take me to the wrestling matches, but, years later, she also took my children to see wrestling.

Over the years we lived in several different apartments and apartment hotels. The first apartment that I really remember was located on Aldine Avenue just west of the lake. As I recall, we lived in that neighborhood, in two or three different apartments, throughout the Depression. It wasn't until years later that I discovered that *Happy Days,'* Tom Bosley, had been an early childhood friend. He was in Chicago and surprised me with a phone call since he had seen an article about my beloved Chicago Sting in the newspapers mentioning my name. And, sure enough, he came out to Wrigley Field that afternoon and saw the Sting. We haven't seen each other since. Maybe he didn't like the Wrigley Field toilets. Hmmm!

I was around 10 years of age when my parents decided to move out of the Lake View neighborhood, further north, to Edgewater. Our first apartment there was located at Thorndale and Winthrop, across from Swift Elementary School. Later we moved to the Grandeur Hotel and then to Winthrop Towers at 6151 North Winthrop. During my summers in the neighborhood I must have spent 18 hours a day at the Swift playground. I began attending Swift School in fourth grade and graduated in January, 1941 as part of a mid-year class before going to Senn High School.

As I look back on my life, I think that everything in those years was centered within an imaginary triangular area that included the Swift School playground, Ardmore Beach, and, later,

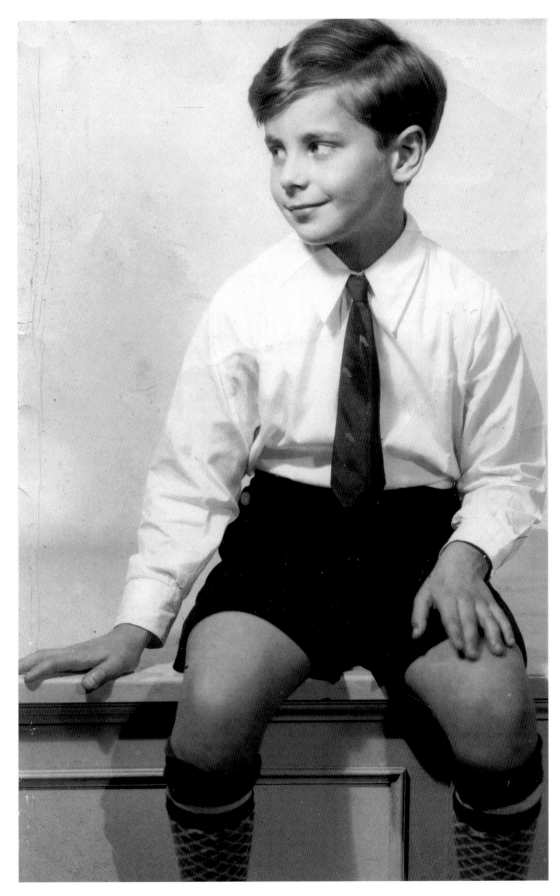

A well-dressed Mr. Stern at age 6, or there abouts.

(L-R), 1935, Cousin Elaine and Jerry Saperston, and yours truly, about 8 years old.

Al's Tick Tock. That was the type of pattern for kids growing up across Chicago during those years: neighborhood schools, playgrounds, parks, and beaches where the kids "lived" while growing up, and local hangouts during high school and college years. Swift School actually had a swimming pool, which made it one of only two elementary schools in Chicago to have such facilities. There were also playgrounds for us on both the north and south sides of the school. One was designated as the girls' playground and the other was technically the boys' playground. We used to play 16-inch softball there and use the field house where we learned to wrestle, play "tug-of-war," and touch football. In the summertime we would compete in sports against other schools from all over the city. As I recall, our biggest competition was against kids who attended Pierce and Hayt Schools located in neighborhoods that were close to us. My favorite sport growing up was 16-inch softball and, in those days, we were part of organized team leagues. I can remember that, starting in fourth or fifth grade, I was a pretty good player, rating myself 7.5 on a scale of 10. We had a great softball team that was sponsored by Simonize, the car polish company, because the father of one of our buddies, Kenny Rich, owned that company and the term "rich" truly applied to him. He was a great guy!

Most of the sports played at Swift were organized, and during all those years I can remember two playground instructors: Fred O'Keefe, who later coached Schurz and became one of Chicago's most successful football coaches; and, Lew Crandal, who was in charge of sports at the schoolyard at Swift, and later became head of the after-school sports program for the Chicago Board of Education.

Touch football was also a big sport for me, and, along with softball, those were our two favorite athletic activities. But, the trouble with playing football, or even baseball, at Swift was that we had to watch where we were running because it was much too easy to run right into the teeter-totters in the playground. That was probably the most dangerous thing in our young lives. I remember that there were also horseshoe pits that were located near the basketball court, and we had to be careful not to run into them and trip. We used to have high school and college guys playing at our schoolyard and some of them, like my friend Buzz Murphy, who was only 5'9", were outstanding players at Senn when they won the city championship. At Swift, Buzz would dribble the basketball around the horseshoe pit and lay the ball up into the basket. The other guys would have to stop defending him rather than run into the pit.

We also had a football team at Swift called the Leathernecks, and we were coached by an ex-Marine. I was only in seventh grade when I started to play tackle football, and I ended up playing tackle football for two years in grammar school, four years at Senn, one year at the University of Illinois, and then one season with the Air Force All Stars in Europe.

Edgewater was really the neighborhood where I spent my formative years, and I can remember so many things about it. For example, I used to sell magazines like the *Saturday Evening Post* and the *Ladies Home Journal* by going door to door. I remember selling newspapers near the Loyola "L" on Sheridan Road when Germany invaded Austria in 1939. I sold a lot of newspapers that day.

Sheridan Road, from the world famous Edgewater Beach Hotel and the Edgewater Beach Apartments northward to Devon Avenue, was a street of beautiful homes and very few apartment buildings. The pier at the Edgewater Beach Hotel extended out into the lake, like a small Navy Pier, and they would have speedboats out there. The Beach Walk was a world-famous place where couples went on dates for dinner and dancing. I remember going there regularly to hear the bandleader Xavier Cugat, as well as many other famous stars of the day. In fact, as a kid, we would sneak around the hotel's protective fence, and when I was older I went there to sip mint juleps and meet young ladies, but that was well before I knew my wife. There was also the Edgewater Beach Tennis Club where Bobby Riggs played tennis. Later on, they built the Edgewater Beach Cabana Club that Norma and I joined during the early 1950s with our late, dear friends Jerry and Betty Nolan who were married on the same day as Norma and me. In grammar school and high school, we spent all summer at the nearby beaches at Hollywood, Ardmore, and Thorndale. We considered those beaches as part of our neighborhood park network.

Growing up, we would go to several neighborhood movie theaters including the Devon Theater on Broadway near Devon, the Bryn Mawr Theater on Bryn Mawr just west of the "L," and the majestic Balaban and Katz Granada Theater on Sheridan Road just north of Devon. There was a parking lot next to the Granada and some of my friends worked there parking cars. Further south of us were the Riviera and Uptown Theaters in Uptown, but we didn't go to the Riviera much because we might end up in fights. I can remember that there were also fights going on at the Granada, although I don't know what they were about. We would also go downtown to the Balaban and Katz Chicago Theater and other downtown movie palaces to see movies and live stage shows.

We had a neighborhood bowling alley called the Glenlake Bowl on Broadway between Glenlake and Granville. In those days automatic lanes didn't exist, but rather the pins were reset after each line by pin boys, usually drunkards who received $.10 a line. Every once in a while, if they didn't have pin boys available, a couple of guys from our group would set the pins. When we bowled, we would try to roll the bowling balls as fast as we could, often before the pins had been reset. We spent a lot of time there before and after World War II.

Neighborhood shopping was concentrated on Granville, Bryn Mawr, and Broadway, but my favorite place, and, in some ways, another center of my neighborhood life, was Al's Tick Tock located on Broadway, on the east side of the street, just north of Thorndale. Al's Tick Tock was the local hangout for high school kids, included about a half dozen booths and counters, and served great sandwiches and milkshakes. By the time I got to Senn High School in 1941, it had become our hangout. It was owned by Al Beskin whose son, Marvin Beskin, attended Sullivan High School where he was a tennis and basketball star: Marvin was the first basketball player in the city to score more than 60 points in a game.

During the years of my youth, parents gave their kids the freedom to roam around the city because there was no perceived fear about allowing their kids such mobility. In fact, I remember that when I was around 12 or 13 years old, I was taking buses all over Chicago by myself or with friends to go places like Wrigley Field, downtown, or Soldier Field to see sporting events. I can still visualize the double-decker, open top buses that moved up and down Sheridan Road and the Outer Drive, but while we did take the "L" downtown, the subway portion of the ride wasn't fully completed until 1943. Then, in high school, I recall going to the Riverview Amusement Park on Belmont and Western, and there were always days during the school year when we would cut classes to go to Riverview.

In terms of baseball, the Cubs were my team. During the '30s and '40s, games began at 3 p.m. in the afternoon when they were playing in Chicago. We would go to the LeMoyne School playground where the Cubs would give out free tickets for the games. Kids lined up because they distributed tickets to sit in the Wrigley Field grandstands and see Cubs games which, at that time, were only played during daylight hours. I was an aggressive kid and used to sneak into the lines of kids from different schools to get more tickets. That move enabled me to see two to three games a week. They used to have color-coded tickets every day, and I collected them because it meant that I could go to the ballpark before each game and find out which tickets they were taking that day. For example, if they were taking red-colored tickets to get to the grandstand, I would take out a red ticket and show it to the usher. Then after I got into the ballpark, I would sneak into the box seat area that was located right next to the baseball diamond. As a result of being a regular at the park, I got to know the famous "40,000 Murphy" (a name derived from his predicting that the attendance at every game was 40,000), and later on, Murphy actually worked for me during the Sting years.

At Wrigley Field I would sneak down to the box seats, and, one day, I was sitting in a front row seat near the screen behind home plate, next to the on-field announcer, Pat Pieper, who was one of my idols. There was an elderly lady who always sat there and she took a liking to me. In those days, when I would go to a game, I never looked liked the kids do today wearing sloppy clothing. I always tried to look nice with a clean shirt and pressed pants. This woman was always very kind to me, and she had two box seat tickets because her son, who was an adult, almost never went to the Cub games. She used to let me sit next to her, and, as a consequence, because I was in the front row, I was privileged to see, up close, such baseball legends as Casey Stengel and Al Lopez as well as many other famous players who were really nice guys.

Many years later, when I became involved with soccer as owner of the Chicago Sting, I got to know Bill Hagenah, Jr., who was president of the Cubs from 1977 to 1981. One day I told him the story about the woman who was so nice to me when I was a kid, and I learned that she was Mrs. Reed, the wife of the owner of Reed Candies. Evidently, Phil Wrigley had bought Reed Candies and that was why Mrs. Reed had such good seats at the ballpark. It took me 25-30 years to learn that story.

I can also remember a time when the Cubs were playing the New York Giants and, Harry Danning, the catcher for the Giants was warming up their starting pitcher before the game. The ball happened to hit his glove and bounce into the stands where I was sitting in

Dad, Mom, and yours truly at the Stork Club, New York City in 1944. Mom was on a buying trip for The Fair Store.

Steve Assimos

My dad, George, and Lee were boyhood friends who first went to Swift School on Thorndale Avenue and became very close, and when they attended nearby Senn High School they played together on the school's football team. Since Dad's family was Greek and Lee's was Jewish they had to deal with a prohibition within the Greek community about Greek girls dating outside the ethnic group. However, my father used to tell us that he was able to have Lee "pass" as a Greek by changing his name to Sternopolis so that they could go on double dates. They were such great friends that it seemed as if they were brothers.

Ever since we were all little kids my brothers, Dean and Billy, always referred to Lee as "Uncle Lee," and still do. In fact, we were closer to him than to even some of my blood relatives. When I look at Lee and Norma's relationship and the closeness of their family, it supports my argument that every successful guy has a good woman behind him. My Dad certainly did, and my mother, Helen, remains very close to Lee and Norma to this day.

I give Lee all the credit for popularizing soccer in Chicago. During an era where Chicago was really struggling with its sports franchises, Lee brought the city two championship teams. In addition, he stayed active in the sport even after closing down the Sting, and was very instrumental in bringing the World Cup to Chicago. The real success of Lee Stern and the best measure of his friendship with my dad was that he always maintained their close friendship, and when Lee bought the Sting franchise, dad didn't miss attending many games. He was always there and very much a fan. To his credit, when my dad got a chance to see his grandchildren play soccer, he was one of the few grandparents who knew the rules.

("Uncle George holding "Dr" Dean and Lee holding Jeffrey, c. 1952

Chapter Two
High School and
The War Years

Lee, at top left, with his Senn High sweeties and close friend Herb Haberstroh, in Fall 1944.

*Lee and Senn High School teammate
Bob Nelson, celebrating New Years Eve,
1945, just before Lee goes to Germany.*

While I was overseas in the military in Germany, my parents had divorced, but I always remained close to both of them. Mom passed away when she was 84 years old. But, just before she died, she had called me about 2 a.m. soon after giving herself an 84th birthday party at the Drake Hotel. She told me that she was having a heart attack and when I asked her how she knew it was a heart attack, her answer was quite simple – "I know it!" She had called the fire department and left the door open to the apartment. When I arrived at her apartment, she was being readied by the paramedics to be transported to Northwestern Memorial Hospital.

Early next morning I visited her and she was sleeping. I went to work, but two hours later, her doctor, Dr. Neil Stone, called me at work and said "Get to the hospital right away." When I arrived, she had just passed away but, I was always thankful that I had been able to see her before she died.

All my kids were with Norma and me at the hospital after she died. While we were still in the room, Irv Kupcinet of the *Chicago Sun-Times* happened to walk by. Kup was an old friend, and my mother loved his column. All of a sudden, all of the kids and Norma and I looked at each other and we started to laugh. How could we possibly laugh under such conditions? Well, we all thought the same thing: my mother would have been so thrilled to know that Kup would have been the first person outside the family to have learned of her death. That's absolutely true!

One of the most interesting aspects of my mother's birthday party had to do with boxes of candy. When she had her birthday party at the Drake, she had brought boxes of candy to be put on the tables. She was arranging all that with the maitre'd, but, for some reason, the candy seemed to have disappeared. Mom became very upset because she believed that somebody had stolen the candy, but I just told her to calm down and forget about it. About two or three days after she had passed away, Norma and I went back to check on her apartment and when we opened the door it was freezing in there. One of the little windows had been left open and when I looked on the window ledge, there were the boxes of candy. She had placed them on the window ledge so that, overnight, they wouldn't

Getting ready to walk down the aisle. My dad is at the extreme right and my father-in-law to be, Louis Retchin, is at the second left. Dick Hartman, my best man, is standing next to me and checking his watch.

*(L-R), Lee, his mother, Tootsie, Simon Wiesenthal famed
Nazi hunter, and Norma, at dinner honoring Mr. Wiesenthal,
c. 1980. We became good friends and had coffee at our
apartment after dinner at Eli's.*

Stern, Jeff's wife, who handles all of the problems that occur because of her father-in-law; and, Ursula, better known as Uli, Kenny's wife, who is the family photographer and the new mother of our youngest grandchild, born January 11, 2010–Samantha, or "Sammie."

Among our grandchildren, the oldest one, Michael, is Vice President of Technology at the Chicago Climate Exchange, 31 years old, and Danny's oldest son. He is a very interesting and hard working guy who went to the University of Oregon, a liberal university. He met his wife, Bree there. She is a lovely gal who is a professional chef and a great sailor. Jan is the mother of twin daughters, Danielle and Rachel, who are 18 years old. Her daughter Michelle, is 16 years old…(all of whom are beauties), and Sampson, her only son and the oldest of her four children, just turned 21 years old, and attends the University of Iowa. He recently spent a summer abroad in Madrid, Spain.

Jeffrey has two sons, the oldest of whom, Scott, is an analyst with the U.S. State Department and married to Leah, a fellow classmate from American University in Washington, DC. She is a professional photographer. Adam, Jeffrey's youngest son graduated from Indiana University, and is now focused on becoming an actor. He is working with one of the top acting schools in New York City. Jeffrey's daughter Alexa, who is 19 years old, is at Penn State University and is in the School of Architecture.

Danny's other son is named David Stern, whose nickname is the "Commissioner"… guess why? He is a Phi Beta Kappa at the University of Texas and recently passed the Illinois Bar Exam after attending the Loyola School of Law in Chicago. He is actively involved in the upcoming Congressional races. Finally, there is Danny's daughter, Jill, who is a clinical psychologist. She is married to an Israeli lawyer, Ilan Shahar. He is presently at Loyola University Law School and is preparing to take the Illinois Bar Exam so that he can practice law in Chicago. He was a first sergeant in the Israeli Army, and his job was to defuse bombs. Wow!

Stern family with Natalie Hoffert, back, to right of Lee, visiting U.S. Congressman Robert McClory (IL), to right of Natalie, in Washington, DC, Summer, 1963 during famous Dr. Martin Luther King rally.

Rancho del Rio, Tucson Arizona, early 1960's. You can't have more fun than we had during these times. Even though the horses may not have enjoyed it!

(L-R), Danny, January, Kenny and Jeffrey at a very, very happy moment at Michael Stern's wedding.

Interviews

I am the oldest of the four Stern kids, born in Chicago in 1951. Although we lived in an apartment in Chicago off of Peterson on Fairfield until I was three years old, I do recall that, for a few months after I was born, the three of us resided in the Sovereign Hotel in the Edgewater neighborhood. In 1955, the family moved to a new, four-bedroom house in Glencoe at 1010 Skokie Ridge and we lived there until I was nine years old and going into fifth grade. My brother Danny was born after we moved into the Fairfield apartment. Then, Jan and Kenny were born after we moved to Glencoe. At that point, the family needed a bigger house for the six of us. Since there were no five-bedroom homes available in Glencoe, we moved to Highland Park. We lived there until I was out of college.

While in Highland Park, I attended Highland Park High School and was active in such sports as football and track. Most of the time I was a running back and defensive back on the football team, although during my junior year, for some unknown reason, they moved me to quarterback. I had never played quarterback before and don't know why they assigned me to that position, but due to injuries and ineligibilities, by the end of the year I was the second-string quarterback.

I became very interested in soccer when the NASL (North American Soccer League) started in 1967, and I began playing the sport at the age of 15. However, there were no soccer programs for us and we didn't have soccer at Highland Park High School. After I graduated from high school in 1969, I attended Cornell University and was able to play intramural soccer in college. In fact, after graduating from Cornell, I wanted to continue playing that sport.

The Chicago Sting began operations in 1975, and when I came back to Chicago after completing an MBA program at the University of Michigan, I chose to play soccer in the Chicago area on a regular basis. I guess that since there were enough guys like me who liked to be active in the sport, we created our own soccer league. But, we didn't want to be connected to any of the existing ethnic teams or pay a lot of money to do it. We ended up with somewhere between 8 to 12 teams around the Chicago area and played during the summers and indoors at Soccer City in Highland Park , one of the first indoor soccer facilities in the northern suburbs. Dad was one of the investors, along with Benny Alon, an Israeli, who played for the Sting.

A few years later, Willy Roy, the Sting coach, had his own soccer facility in Dolton and I ended up also playing there. Willy referred to us as his "house team," which included Willy, his three sons who were in high school at the time, my brothers Kenny, and Danny (who never played soccer before), me, Sam Der-Yeghiyian, and various other people. When they had an odd number of teams we would make it an even number, but Willy said that we were not allowed to win the championship. I played there until I was in my 30s, but since we were living in the city, I got tired of driving to Dolton at 8 p.m. to play soccer. Years later, since the time when my oldest son started playing the sport at the age of 5, I have been involved in AYSO (American Youth Soccer Organization).

I was not active at the Sting like my younger brother, Kenny, although there occasionally were some things that I would do to help my dad and the team. I would go to the games regularly, just like most of the family, and once in a while I would attend out-of-town games.

I became involved in the business of trading at the Board of Trade before I began graduate school. About the time I was a senior at Cornell, my father had to have two memberships for clearing purposes at his firm, Lee B. Stern and Company, and the second membership was listed under Uncle Bernie, who had the membership and worked for him. However, Dad told me that he wanted to change the membership out of Uncle Bernie's name. His intention was to put it in my name when I became 21 years old and it didn't matter whether I ever actually used it. Although I didn't know at the time what I wanted to do after college, Dad encouraged me to go to business school, and I ended up being accepted at the University of Michigan. I came home for the summer between undergraduate and graduate school, got the membership at the Board of Trade, and came downtown to see if I liked trading or was interested at all in doing it.

At first, like all new traders who were scared to even open their mouths on the floor, it was pretty tough. But, as the summer progressed and I was brought into the silver pit by some of the brokers, I learned how to fill orders. Then I began business school, and when I came home during the summer between my two years at Michigan, I traded some more. I returned to Michigan to complete business school, and by then, all my classmates were applying for jobs. It was the fall of 1974 and, at that time, the economy was terrible. During the second year of my MBA program I started thinking about what I might want to do for a career, and the only thing I could think of was to seek a position at a bank doing trading. But, I realized that it made no sense to look for a job elsewhere since I could just work at the Board of Trade and really do what interested me. That was when I really realized trading was what I wanted to do for a career.

I started full-time at the Board in the summer of 1975 and was on the floor in various pits from that point until late 1989. Each time I considered "leaving the floor" before then, I always went back, and it has now been more than 35 years since I began as a full-time trader as a way of making a living. In our office we trade for ourselves, and all of us have earned our living through our own trades over the years.

As for my dad, his personality and style have a lot to do with why he has been so successful in a way that doesn't seem to work for anybody else. He is a very "shoot from the hip" kind of guy and tends to just react to things. Sometimes his reactions cause me to cringe, but his style of trading seems to be based on this even if he has to quickly change his mind later about some decisions. He has a "trader" mentality which people don't understand because it seems to be based on being impulsive, but it's really more than that. One thing you have to do in trading is if you are in a bad trade, you just get out, and Dad is one of the quickest guys to get out. I don't think that ego gets in the way of his decisions since he just gets out and then feels a lot better.

His trading style now is something he can't explain. He just knows what to do after being down here for 60 years, and sometimes doesn't seem to appreciate the fact that other people don't understand situations the same way. My style is to analyze everything I do because that is just the way I operate. Over the years, I have had to try different things and I kind of know myself, in terms of trading, that I can't trade like my dad. He might moan and groan when he has had a losing day, but then he moves right on. He treats each day separately and wants to know at the close of trading how much he made and how much he lost. I keep saying to him to look at investments over a period of time–a month or a year. But, he doesn't look for a percentage gain or loss because he only wants to know how many dollars he has made.

The classic story from my brother Danny is that, one time, Dad wanted to invest in something that would produce income for him. So, Danny made an investment recommendation. Shortly afterwards, my father sold it at a profit. Danny said to him, "I thought that you wanted something that was income producing?" Dad said, "I made money, so that's income." That style is why he is successful down here. Maybe some of it could be explained by the era of the '30s and '40s when he grew up, but most of it can be explained by just the way he is.

As for his years owning the Sting, I can remember that during those days there were times when he would yell at his head coach, Willy Roy, or some of the newspaper guys. To him, that was his reaction to the situation even if he might have to apologize afterward. I can tell you that you don't want to be the next person with whom he comes in contact because you will be the recipient of his anger even though you are not the person at whom he is mad. As for his kids, sometimes he would get angry at us not because of something we did, but rather because he might have lost money that day. He just reacts and then, sometimes, he has to backtrack because he is getting it out of his system.

His reputation at the Board of Trade is very good because of his business sense and ability as a trader, and I think that he is considered one of the great ones. There are some people here who will say that he is the best they have ever seen, but Dad says that about other people, too. When he would come into the pit to make a trade, people often assumed that he knew something or something must be happening and they would mimic his actions. I am sure that there may be a level of jealousy toward him, but I have never seen it demonstrated. Whatever he made at the Board, he did on his own, although he did have some great mentors in his career. However, he figured it out his own way while taking advantage of advice from others.

The Board of Trade has always been a cliquey place, but Dad was lucky enough to have mentors who helped bring him along, people like Stubby Sachs and Herman Gordon. On the other hand, I am not sure that he has been a mentor to others in the same way, although he has levels of concern about people at the Board and has always been willing to give advice and help people. His mentors were brokers and they could bring somebody in and teach them the ways. But, like Dad, as a trader myself, I find it hard to explain to people how to do something.

If I were describing my dad to somebody who didn't know him, I would say that he is very devoted to his family. He always wants to know the details about the lives of his

The gang (minus Samantha Stern, born January 11, 2010 and Ilan Shahar, Jill's husband) at Kenny and Uli's wedding, Chicago, Illinois 2007.

children and grandchildren. His integrity is also very important and he wants to do the right thing, even if it costs him money. A good example was the Sting because a lot of guys in that situation would have just closed the doors and not paid their bills. Dad would never have done that. He gets upset if people suggest that he folded the franchise or that it went defunct. He says, "No, we didn't. We just closed the business and paid all our bills."

Dan Stern

I was born in Chicago in 1953 and lived with my parents and Jeffrey in the apartment on Peterson for two years. But I really grew up first, in Glencoe, and then, for the most part, in Highland Park. We lived in Glencoe from 1955 to 1961, and I attended Highland Park High School, graduating from there in 1971. I always had an interest in sports. I was a Cubs fan while Jeff was a Sox fan. Jeff, probably doesn't remember that one day in the 1950s when we were living in Glencoe, my father brought home two uniforms. I grabbed the White Sox uniform and Jeff said, "No, I want the Sox uniform!" I said, okay, fine, and I took the Cubs uniform. Being a lifelong Cubs fan, 1969 really hurt because the Cubs just broke my heart and after that it was just never the same. However, when my father bought into the White Sox, I channeled some of my Chicago baseball interest into the Sox. Today I am more of a White Sox fan than a Cubs fan. As I just said, it was never the same after 1969.

Growing up, I was never interested in soccer and didn't play the sport. When the North American Soccer League started in the United States in either 1966 or 1967, Jeff went to the Highland Park Recreation Center and talked to Mr. Carlson, who was in charge of the Center. That led to the start of soccer in Highland Park. Jeff used to have all these soccer games on the front lawn with friends, but I never played because I was focusing on football, which was my sport in high school. My father used to say to me, "Danny, I will make you into a great center on your football team like I was at Senn High School." But, instead, I was a running back at Highland Park High School as well as playing what they called, at that time, offensive end. Today, no one knows what that position is or was. I also played defense in the secondary.

After high school, I attended the University of Arizona where I majored in psychology, graduating from there in 1975. That subject comes in handy now that I have a career in trading because psychology is more of a mind-set than anything else, and it really helps in trading. For one thing, when you trade, you have to leave all of your emotions and issues somewhere else or you will end up losing money.

I was a Board of Trade member beginning in 1974, so on vacations from college I used to trade a little bit and execute orders with my cousin, Keith Bronstein, in the soybean pit. I began working for Lee B. Stern and Company when I was 16 years old, going there every summer and every winter. I would say that it provided me with a great education, not just what happens on the trading floor but also what goes on in the back office.

In terms of my father's influence on my career, he never said too much about it, except to tell me, "You're the boss, and the hours are great." Back in the 1960s, life was simpler and we didn't worry as much about careers as people do today. I see the process that my children have gone through to get jobs and it certainly is different.

People ask me every day what my father taught me as a trader: never risk more than 20% of one's net worth; and, take quick losses. With him, a lot of it was a combination of instincts and capital preservation. I know that one day, the call on beans was $.20 lower and that was a big drop. Dad was in the office about the time that I was going to the trading floor and he said to me, "Buy the opening!" I said to him, "Well, it's going to be $.20 lower." He said to me, "That's too cheap, so just buy it." Since I am more analytical than instinctual, I questioned his suggestion. He repeated, "Danny, just buy it because it is cheap." So, it opened $.20 lower at $5.80 but quickly rallied to $5.85. I thought to myself, "Dad's right, I'm going to go buy it." I paid $5.85 but that was the top and I took a loss. I said to him, "I lost money." He asked me whether I had bought at the opening. I said, "No, just after. I paid $5.85." His answer was, "$5.85...that's where I was selling it." Dad's trading modus operandi to a great extent is his DNA.

He gave me my start in trading when he said to me, "Take these corn orders and go execute them." That gave me a sense for how to conduct myself in a pit and how to execute trades. I relied on my experiences gained by working for Lee B. Stern, and Company including the fact that I learned the names of the members, the clearing firms, and how to endorse an order and fill out a trading card. So, I was aware of all the basics that they teach you in the programs at the Board for new members. It meant that by the first day I was trading I was comfortable...I didn't know what I was doing, but I was still comfortable because I could put a trade down on my cards.

As for being a Stern at the Board, the influence it has for us is that we seem to automatically get a lot of respect along with a certain degree of jealousy. There are clearly people who dislike me because they probably dislike my father, but although he is a little bit controversial, he is not political at all. He has always said exactly what he wanted to say, which means that he might have stepped on some toes...but that is fine with me. I figure that those people who don't like me because of my dad are irrelevant because I don't want to be with them and I couldn't care less. Clearly, the advantages of being a Stern far out-weigh the disadvantages, and it is funny to me that there are a lot of people at the Board in their 30s and 40s who keep calling me "Mr. Stern." I don't know who some of them are but I appreciate the compliment.

My father got involved in sports because he was apparently looking for something to do outside of his trading business. He has always been a sports fan, and, at one time, he wanted to be a newspaper reporter (his joke was, "I'm not Stern from the Trib...I'm brown from the Sun") so being a sports team owner was a step up from being a newspaper reporter. He tried to buy the New Orleans Saints, and that would have been wonderful considering their value today, but the deal didn't get too far. He was looking for an NFL team to buy, and, in those days, teams cost a lot of money. But it just didn't work out. I didn't know much about soccer until the summer of 1974 when Phil Woosnam, the

(L-R), Norma, Lee and January.
Three youngsters getting ready for
a sea voyage, c. 1985.

Commissioner of the North American Soccer League (NASL), was visiting our office one afternoon. Dad said to me, "Danny, come on in and sit down." I listened to their conversation for about an hour, and later I asked my father, "What was that all about?" since he hadn't mentioned anything to me. He said that he was thinking about buying a soccer team, and I was surprised since we had never discussed it. However, I thought that it was a pretty good idea.

After that I went back to school, and he told me that he had gone to the Soccer Bowl and had met Kyle Rote and Lamar Hunt. I didn't pay that much attention to it because I was in Tucson enjoying college. The next thing I heard from him was that he had bought a soccer franchise. I remember being home when he told me that he was hiring Bill Foulkes as the coach of his new team. I asked him who Bill Foulkes was, and he told me he was a former captain of Manchester United and a famous English player but said it was a secret that would be announced at a press conference the following week. I didn't understand why he was breaking the news about Bill Foulkes previous to the press conference. Now I understand public relations, and this is how it works. Bill was a very impressive man and it was the beginning of the Sting and a fun time for Dad and the rest of the family.

I went back to college and missed the first couple of games. When I got back, it was freezing outside but still fun to watch the Sting play and see a team that actually belonged to my father. I didn't get involved in any way with the Sting because I was busy trading and had just gotten married. In 1978, my youngest brother, Kenny, became active as the "color man" on television broadcasts. In later years, when they were playing indoor soccer, Kenny became team president. I also remember going to games on Sunday nights. They were so exciting that I didn't want to go to work on Mondays because I was so tired. Family is very important to my father, and when the kids were younger my mother would say to Dad, "Look, you're done at work at 1:15 p.m. Just make sure to be home at 6:30 p.m. every night to play with the kids." When I was little, and we were living in Glencoe, he would come home and sometimes be so tired that he didn't really want to play with us because he wanted to take a nap. I think that I would just lie on his back and fall asleep. He liked that and I liked that. In later years, he would come home and we would play sports like football and baseball. That was always nice and he would take us to many sports events and create fun times for all of us.

As a part-owner of the White Sox, Dad works closely with Jerry Reinsdorf on the team's board of directors. I remember one year that they had a meeting and were deciding to cut the team's budget. In the middle of the meeting, Roland Hemond came in the office and said, "Well, I want to tell you all that we just bought Tom Seaver!" That was the end of the meeting and the budget cutting. I have been told that Reinsdorf has said to the directors, "Each of you has one vote. I've got one vote. The only difference is that my vote counts more." Jerry is the managing partner, but my dad can pick up the phone and talk to Jerry to discuss whatever is on his mind about the team. But, when it comes to final decisions, Jerry is going to do what he wants to do.

A very special picture with January and 2005 World Series Championship trophy.

I would describe my father to people who don't know him as a little hot headed and controversial. But, he is very honest and that is most important to him. He has said, "You are born with a name and you die with that name, so don't screw it up!" His reputation and his family are the two things that are most important to him.

My dad has an old friend named Henry Mautner, someone he has been close to for 50 years since the days living in Glencoe. I remember that on a few occasions they would be going to sports events, and sometimes there would be a traffic situation where a policeman would stop my father for going into a parking lot where he had the correct parking pass, and Dad would "really let him have it." Poor Henry would just sit there and laugh because he had seen this for 50 years. But Dad wasn't afraid of anybody. The funny thing is that, underneath it all, my father is a sweet, gentle kind of guy. He may get into an argument with anybody but he forgets it in a second.

He has four offsprings and is very proud of all of us but in different ways because we are each unique individuals. He definitely loves my mother a lot. They have been married all these years and probably look at each other the same way they did when they first met. I think that is really nice because I think they have a model marriage.

January Stern

I was born on March 23, 1956 and lived in Glencoe until I was about 4 or 5 years old before we moved to Highland Park. I attended Highland Park High School, a challenging experience at a challenging time in our society, when the whole high school paradigm from the top down suddenly shifted. And yes, the city seemed vastly more interesting and realistic than the suburban life. My first year of college at Tulane University in New Orleans lacked personal focus, so I returned to Chicago. My creative soul found me attending both the School of the Art Institute and Columbia College in Chicago. Art, music, photography, philosophy, and astrological sciences were my direction. And—I also started working as a runner at the Board of Trade. When I was younger, I had no direct experience and spent very little time at the Board itself.

Growing up, this institution was a constant topic of discussion within my family. We'd sit at the dinner table, and my dad would give a rendition of his trading that day. I really didn't understand exactly what my dad was doing. He talked a lot. First, he was long the 'no-corn' than he was short the 'jan-beans'(I sort of liked anything to do with the "Jan Beans," a convoluted sense of garnering attention, I suppose). Then there was some sort of spread thing going on. My dad kept 'changing his mind' and it was pretty hard to follow. Then he was finished talking and got up from the table, only to return with a lit cigar. There was a great emphasis on numbers and soybeans, and other farm crops! We lived nowhere near a farm as far as I could tell. It made no sense to me as he went to work in Chicago, in an office building, and I didn't understand where they would put these giant bushels of corn, wheat and oats! And what were soybeans? What bothered me a lot, though, was the fact that women were not allowed to participate in what seemed to be any meaningful manner.

I sensed something was seriously awry with that one. Later on though, women were permitted onto the floor and allowed to engage in the commerce that was taking place.

I didn't love that part of the business as my father does, and, growing up, I didn't have any friends whose families were in the business. It was an unusual career, and I never fully comprehended what it was except that there were a lot of men yelling at each other all the time. In fact, one of my earliest memories was when I was about three years old around Christmas. I recall standing in the gallery at the Board of Trade with my mom looking at the trading floor and seeing all of these men wearing suits and hats looking like they were in this huge rumble, just yelling and screaming. I thought to myself, was this some sort of mysterious athletic event characterized by a lot of pushing, shoving, yelling, and heated disputes? I couldn't figure out what was going on and didn't understand why they were yelling so much, especially the fact that the noise would quickly cease when the bell rang, signaling the end of the session. It was just so chaotic...and then it stopped.

Now, I didn't necessarily have a desire to trade, but I soon discovered that what my dad was doing was extremely fascinating. Working as a runner on the floor of the Board of Trade provided a great learning environment and insight into my dad and his world. I wasn't necessarily the most practical person at that time, extremely responsible, but not necessarily practical. I simply found the futures industry as an amazing business from a theoretical perspective. Since I loved to travel, the foreign currency and IMM (International Monetary Markets) caught my fancy. I ended up working on the floor of the CME (Chicago Merchantile Exchange) for about a year or so as my dad had a small business there. It was the time when the IMM was just starting out and trading was strictly done off of a blackboard, and there was no pit trading. I was around 20 years old at that time and one could just walk up to the board and say, "Board marker, I'd like to buy 10 Deutschmarks at this price." Someone would come up and say that they would buy the10 D-Marks, and it was simply trading off a blackboard. I decided that I could do it because one wasn't required to have physical dominance. I became a member of the IMM in 1977 and within a month, we started pit trading. This was not good, but I thought OK, I'll give it a shot. While I was bright, intuitive, and perceptive, I was not necessarily outwardly competitive by nature, a definite detriment to successful pit trading. I married and divorced a few years later, and had taken some time away from trading, yet was always watching things from the sidelines, not really being directly involved. It is an incredible and fascinating business that is a male-dominated industry characterized by a lot of chauvinistic and harassing behavior and a lot of fun as well, providing great fodder for future creative endeavors. Thankfully, a lot has changed since I last worked on the floor. I experienced some moderate success, but it wasn't consistent. I really didn't stay there long enough to fully develop my business.

I remarried, and raised four kids, so that was a huge thing because part of what I wanted to do was to have a family. I am now a single mom with four great adult children. Over the years my personal interests have been focused on art, athletics and trend cycles.

Currently, I am a founding partner in a company involved in entertainment projects with traditional and new media.

As for my brothers, they are great, pretty solid, and all different. They were always involved in something that looked fun, and as a little girl, I wanted to join them in whatever they were doing. Despite that, I felt like an outsider growing up. I constantly heard them being told to be careful with me because I was a girl. There were a lot of things that were conveyed to me as being inaccessible due to my female status. I just didn't get it. I wasn't real pleased with their attitudes. I had a better sense about myself than my parents' imposed daughter category. My brothers always were doing something athletic, and fun, and I've always considered myself to be a competent athlete, probably the best natural athlete in the family.

My father has had a great influence on me. Like my father, I've been told I am a bit of a character. But who isn't? I am basically introverted, while I think that my dad is really quite extroverted. Like my Dad, I really try to do the right thing. These are moral and ethical considerations, not simply legal issues. I think that dad is a grounded individual, a responsible person, and very, very creative and spontaneous. If someone watched my dad and then me, it would be easier for an outsider to say if we are alike.

My father is both simple and complex, which I guess sounds conflicted. When I was a little girl, I was definitely scared of him because he yelled a lot. I think it was fortunate for him that he found the right profession where he could do that yelling. Or perhaps, his manner of high-level decibel communication was a direct result of his chosen profession. He's kind of gruff, but Dad was always doing interesting things, and looking back, I remember thinking that he had a funny sense of humor. However, when he would talk to me as a parent, it wasn't fun and not nearly as cool. He was very protective of me, overbearing at times, and I believe a little guilt-ridden, as he wasn't really clear what to do with me. I was "foreign"...a female child unit. As his only daughter, he has, at times, been very awkward with me. Sometimes he appears to be astounded at some of the things I have done and can do. At this point in my life, I find it pretty funny that he finds himself surprised by me. For example, a couple of years ago, I simply drove into the city to meet my parents for dinner, and they were amazed that I drove downtown by myself. I found that to be almost unbelievable. Yet, I did and do recognize how much he tries. I admit I may be a little tough on him, but he is coming from his heart, and I am very thankful for that.

I think that, over the years, I have probably become more comfortable with myself, and, as a result, more comfortable with Dad. My dad doesn't have one shy bone in his body, and that can describe me when I meet new people. He loves the work he does including trading, sports, and investing in art. I would describe him as a character who is funny, bright, and very savvy. He's got a great heart and is very generous, and I respect that he sometimes takes on responsibilities that he doesn't need to because, in his mind, he wants to do the right thing. His word and his reputation are important to him, and he stressed that to us while we were growing up. Dad is a very strong family man and comes

The plaque tells it all. Be'er Sheva, Israel.

from a place in time and context that is different than myself, leading to natural clashes for us to work through.

I couldn't figure out how I ended up in this family because my parents and brothers actually felt foreign to me. Sometimes I actually thought—no, I was convinced that I was adopted, and I wasn't being told. It wasn't until I had my first child that I remember phoning my parents about two months afterward and making a blanket and sincere apology: "I'm so sorry for anything I ever did as a teenager!"

I am proud and thankful for my parents. They are an amazing couple, and my dad wouldn't be who he is without my mom, and I give her tremendous credit for that fact. They are very fortunate to have found each other, and I am lucky to have had that modeled for me without realizing it. Life's experience yields a perspective that can only be made real through the years of living.

Kenny Stern

I was born in 1957 when the family was living in Glencoe. We moved to Highland Park when I was about four- or five-years-old, and I am the youngest of the four. I went to Highland Park High School where I played soccer, and after high school, I attended Southern Methodist University (SMU) in Dallas where I also played soccer until I blew out my knee during my junior year. After graduating from SMU, in 1979 I returned to Chicago and immediately went to work on the floor of the Chicago Board of Trade. I was also involved with the Chicago Sting at that time and throughout its existence.

During 1978–1985, I had worked as an analyst on the Chicago Sting telecasts and broadcast for various radio and television stations. In 1985, I accepted a full-time position with the Sting and served as vice president, President and General Manager through 1988.

I also have been what most would consider a trader over the past 30 years. The word "trader" has different connotations in today's world, and when people think about that work, they tend to think of someone as being a "day trader," someone who is in and out of the market many times a day. I have considered my role to relate more as a speculator than trader in both commodities and equities.

There were two different companies that we operated as we remained involved in soccer following the end of the Sting in 1988. As opportunities came along, the U.S. Soccer Federation and the folks from World Cup '94 inquired about us being involved. Two companies were created that dealt separately with different projects: Soccer International, Ltd; and, 94 Sports Marketing (where Dad was partnered with one of our former players, Benny Alon).

I moved to Las Vegas in 1995 and have remained involved with both the futures/ equities business and professional soccer industry. I also finished a long-time project, the novel "Kicks," which had become a huge part of my life and a great source of my energies.

I have nothing but warm and proud memories about being a member of the Stern family. The four siblings have always been close to each other, and that related to a strong family environment. I felt fortunate growing up with both parents, and no matter how busy they were, at all times they prioritized their kids as first and foremost.

My father has a strong personality and is someone who gives a lot to his family and friends—and those family and friends are always eager to reciprocate. I think one way to understand Dad is that he has always treated his businesses, including his soccer team, with a customer-friendly priority. When he operated the Sting he wasn't comfortable if the fans weren't happy, he felt that he wasn't doing enough for them, or that the team they were supporting wasn't good enough at that time. On the other hand, when the fans were happy and the team was playing well, he was happiest knowing that he was providing as best he could for his "customers." Over 14 years of existence, the times his customers were happy heavily outweighed the times the effort came up short—which is a great testament to the time and effort he put into the Chicago Sting.

In my opinion, the same general approach has also related to how he has very successfully run his company at the Chicago Board of Trade.

I cannot imagine there have been many people that cared as much about their employees. I was always amazed at how important the Chicago Sting players were to him, and I think that the players knew that as well. He has always taken his relationships with family, employees (including his players), and even fans as something very personal. He has 11 grandchildren, and all of his children and grandchildren continue to be incredibly important to him. One aspect of Dad's personality is that he is driven by the need to keep up with what is happening with all grandchildren on any given day. Some people think that if most of their family does well it is fantastic. But, if only one of his grandkids is not doing "fantastic" in his mind, then it bothers Dad and he will stay awake thinking how he might effectively involve himself in the situation.

I think that the way he grew up in his neighborhood has had an impact on what my father has accomplished, and his perspective on life has helped him greatly in dealing with success. He has never forgotten his life growing up as well as when things weren't as easy as later on times when he became financially successful. From that respect, I think that growing up the way he did relates to how his life has developed and growing up in an old-time neighborhood environment strongly and positively impacted him. Dad was an only child, but I can't imagine any siblings, anywhere in the world, having a closer relationship than he did with his long-time friend, George Assimos. That obviously evolved from Dad's neighborhood roots since he and my "Uncle George" first met at the Swift Elementary School playground.

My father is a very sensitive person which can at times be masked by the outward behavior of a tough businessman. As for similarities between us, there is very much in common—I hope—one common trait that jumps out might be a strong overlap related to a similar sense of humor. My humor is what I would consider to be very dry—very, very "dry," —but Dad can quickly pick up on some of the things that I am saying, and I probably enjoy that a lot. At times I get frustrated when I have to clarify to others that I am joking

Mama and Papa with January's twins,
Rachel and Danielle, 1992.

*(L-R), Kenny, LBS and cousin Ira Eichner
at Kenny's pre-wedding party, 2007.*

or kidding about things. But, I never have to explain it to Dad. He'll enjoy it or not enjoy it very, very quickly. I also think that my father is sensitive to the different personalities of his children, although I'm not sure that we ever gave him a chance or a choice. That trait was probably developed from a standpoint of survival.

Ira Eichner

Lee and I have been very close personal friends and business associates for many years as well as cousins since his father and my mother were first cousins. He is a guy that the more you know him, the more you love him. He's warm, outspoken, has a great sense of humor, is a very loyal, caring person, and, if you are a friend of his, he will always go the distance for you. I think of Lee as a family man and an all-around good guy.

I can remember when he was in a ticker tape parade downtown that the city held for the champion Sting team after it won the Soccer Bowl in 1981. It was a hell of a big thing to have the mayor of Chicago riding in the parade with him and the people of Chicago throwing flowers at Lee. Although he is in his early 80s, Lee has more energy today than anyone else I know who is that age. He is fun and a sport and the first guy to reach in his pocket if somebody needs any help. He has had his ups and downs with some of his business dealings, but Lee is a consummate trader and always ends up on the top of the pile. My business background was as chairman and founder of the AAR Corporation from which I retired in 2005. The company began as an aircraft parts business and then provided maintenance services for large airlines and the military. Lee was a member of the board of directors of AAR for about 15 years, and I always valued his advice.

Chapter Four
At The Board of Trade

The story of how I ended up having a 60-year career at the Chicago Board of Trade actually began when I was at Swift Elementary School and our class was taken on a field trip to the Board of Trade. In addition, there was a man who lived upstairs from my aunt and uncle who was a member of the Board of Trade, and it meant that I knew the place existed, probably unlike most of the other 2.5 million people living in Chicago. However, at that time in my life, I never thought about coming to work at the Board.

When I was honorably discharged from the Air Force in February 1947, I worked at Blue Cross for a couple of months, but that wasn't my stuff. Then I went to work in the front office of the Chicago Cubs. I had sent them copies of newspaper articles I had written while serving in the military and they hired me, sight unseen and without any inside connections. Sadly, I was "released" by the Cubs after being there just six months of working as the assistant to the assistant general manager of the club, Harold George. At that time, I hadn't met my wife-to-be, Norma, so I thought about going to school at the University of Miami. I had received a letter from the football coach of Miami University, Andy Gustafson, who invited me to come to the university and try out for the football team. I didn't need a scholarship because of the GI Bill, so that made us "cheap fodder." I flew down there and when I got off the plane, and was looking around, I saw two young ladies in an automobile. Since I didn't know where the university was located. I asked them if they knew where the university was at. They responded, "Sure, we'll drive you over there." I got in the car but never did get to the campus and never saw the university until many, many years later. As things turned out later, I finished three years of college: half a year at the University of Illinois; and, two and a half years at Roosevelt College.

Since I had completed my military service and the job with the Cubs had ended, I decided to return to college and think about my future. In fact, I thought that it would be kind of nice to take afternoon classes so that I would be able to sleep a little later in the morning. In addition, it provided an opportunity to go out late at night, although I didn't have that much money since we were only receiving $75 a month from the government.

On the second floor of Roosevelt College was the student lounge as well as the employment office, and, ironically, if those two places had not been located next to each other, I probably wouldn't have found the employment office. One day, I saw a sign on the board announcing that there were positions available as runners at the Board of Trade with work hours of 9:15 a.m. to 1:30 p.m.

My classes started at 1:50 p.m., the jobs were paying $25 a week, and that sounded pretty good since it would add $75–$100 a month to what I was already receiving from the government. A runner took orders on the floor and brought them back to the broker via telephoned order clerks to the brokers in the pit. It didn't take too many brains to do the job, and, as I found out later, most of the guys down there didn't have any brains to begin with. So, I got the job, began making $175 a month, ended up with a few of the brokers sorting their orders, and that was worth an extra $25 a month. So, in 1947, if you were making $200 a month, you were a wealthy, young guy and the job was kind of fun. I would always hitchhike down to school from the North Side since hitchhiking was the common *modus operandi* of travel in those days.

My job at the Board involved me working for Merrill Lynch, and one day I went in to see if I could get a raise because I had been a runner for six or seven months. While at the Board, I noticed that they had about 10 runners. I was the only one who was consistently available, and there was a large turnover in the runners working for the firm. I went to the office manager at Merrill Lynch (a Mr. Stern to whom I was not related) who handled the runners, to ask him for a raise. After explaining to him why I should make more money, and although he was very kind to me, he said, "The bottom line, Lee, is that we pay runners $25 a week. We appreciate your loyalty, but that is all a runner gets." So, when I saw that I wasn't going to make more money there, I decided that it was probably time to look for employment with another firm.

As it turned out, I went to work for Clement Curtis, which was later E.F. Hutton, and since the phone man there also handled another firm that had very little business, they would pay an extra $20 a month just to run their few orders. The bottom line was that instead of getting just $25 a week, I was being paid $30 and $35 a week. I decided that I liked the business and I took a Board of Trade course that was available. A few members took a liking to me, including Herman Gordon, who was my "godfather" down there, and "Stubby" Sachs, as well as Howard Hinman, the floor manager at Merrill Lynch.

When I decided that it might be a good idea to get a membership/seat at the Board (membership was around $2,500 at that time), I talked to my mother about it. She had some war bonds and was working at that time. I also talked to my dad about it, too, but he didn't have any extra funds available. My mother always had confidence in me, but she asked me, "If you buy the membership, what happens if things don't go well? Can you get your money back?" I said, "Well, it all depends on the price of the membership. Generally speaking, I don't think that I would have a problem selling the membership and getting

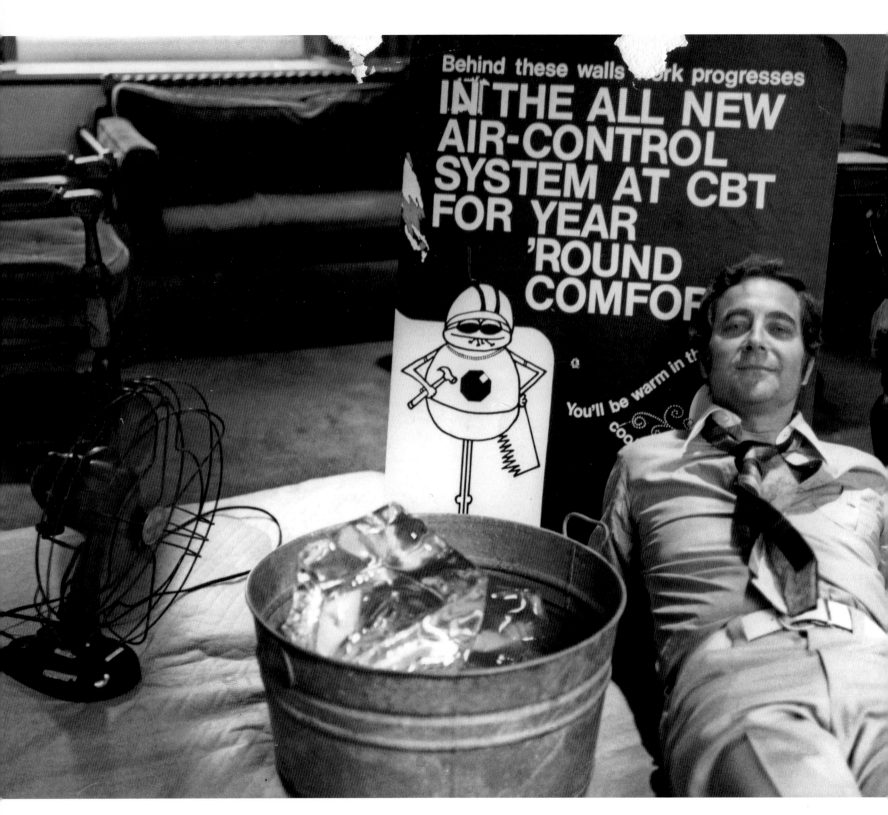

No air conditioning in the middle of summer.
This is the best we could do with the equipment
available, c. 1980.

most of my money back." So, she gave me (she didn't lend it to me) the $2,200 because I already had some money saved from Service.

In order to buy the membership, you needed to be sponsored for a total of $10,000, and Stubby Sachs and Howard Hinman both agreed to sponsor me. Meanwhile, "Stubby" wasn't doing too well in the market. So another member, Milt Kirschbaum, who became a good friend, had to guarantee Stubby who was guaranteeing me, and that made for an interesting, if complicated situation.

Having a membership (seat) allowed me to be a broker on the trading floor, and then I could either trade from my own account or be a broker. I wanted to try to trade from my own account...I had about $500. Things were quite different in those days. The market ranges were very narrow, and $6.25 was considered a move. Being a broker, you would get business from Merrill Lynch or Continental Grain since you needed to trade through a company. Some of the men down there suggested that I talk to John McCarthy, who was a former president of the Board of Trade, an elected office. I went up to Mr. McCarthy and I told him that a couple of people had recommended that I talk to him to see if I could open an account. I said, "Mr. McCarthy, I only have $500." He looked me right in the eye, and said, "Son, if you have more, you may lose it!" So, I opened the account for $500.

I thought to myself, what was the worst that could happen to me? Simply put, the worst thing would be that I lost the $500 and my investment in the seat of $2,500: a total investment of $3,000. The Board of Trade was all commodities: wheat, corn, soybean futures. That was how I started, and I traded small. Since Mr. McCarthy was such a wonderful man he told me that if I got into any financial difficulty, which would have been very, very minor, he was always there to back me up. Later on, when John got sick, I took over the company and that was how Lee B. Stern & Company, the business I have today, got started. Thus, I took over an active company that had floor traders, and most everybody stayed with me. I opened my own company in 1967 and was a member of the clearing-house. The purpose of the company was really to provide me with the ability to trade and not have it cost me any money. A lot of us started small companies that way because we were traders, and, said to ourselves that if we could acquire a few steady customers and some fellow members with whom to trade, then we could cover the cost of trading.

During my career at the Board of Trade I suffered two major crises, none of which had to do with my own trading. The first one was during the big silver market debacle of 1979-82 when Bunker Hunt was attempting to corner the silver market. I had a customer who had suffered a tremendous loss due to the Hunts' attempt to corner the market. It created a technical situation that was unheard of as far as the market was concerned. The trader, who was an important customer and a good friend, and who had $2.5 million in collateral, went broke as a result. Fortunately I was able to weather the storm. We were major players on the silver market as an arbitrage company between New York and Chicago, and it was a very profitable venture. Unfortunately, the silver market as a trading vehicle took on a name of its own. However, thanks to the assistance of the late Ralph

Peters and some of my fellow members, I was able to liquidate the silver position causing all of the problems...but not before my pockets were "slightly emptied out." One thing I've learned over the years is to never put good money after bad when it comes to trying to get your money back after a bad trade or after a horrific problem like this. Fortunately, the following year, I had one of my best trading years ever. I never attempted to get back the money that was lost, but just continued to trade with my own regular style, and the results were more than satisfactory.

The interesting part of the silver debacle was that when Norma and I left for Europe on a two-week vacation, there was a problem not just with the positions of our company but with almost everybody in the silver industry. I had met with the Business Conduct Committee and Bobby Goldberg, who was chairman, and I told him that I had made arrangements for any financial problems if they occurred. He said, "That's fine, Lee." But, when we got to Europe, it was obvious that even though the markets were going up the limit every day, the spreads were out of line. They couldn't move, so there was no money being called by the clearing corporation except for the fact that we knew there were losses occurring which weren't being reflected in the clearing corporation's calls. We were in Sardinia when I heard about this, but there were only one or two planes out of Sardinia and we were trying to make arrangements to fly the Concorde back to the U.S. from London. It was important for me to get back because, at that point, I didn't know whether or not I was broke. As it turned out, I hadn't lost all my money!

The second crisis, and probably the best known, was the infamous bond fiasco of 1992. It happened when two members of the Exchange, one of whom was a new customer of ours, along with a friend of his who had just become a member the day before, and a customer of Goldenberg, Hehmeyer Co., did a scam act on the floor of the Exchange illegally trading Treasury bonds and options. Norma and I were flying down to Florida on October 22, 1992 because we had just built a new house and this was going to be our first weekend in that house. In those days, there were no telephones on the airplanes, and when I arrived in Florida, I turned on my cell phone and called the office to see how things were going. My secretary, Ann Tully, didn't sound quite right to me. I asked her, "Is something the matter?" She responded, "You better talk to Danny." He got on the phone and said to me, "There is a major problem that has happened on the Exchange, and it is a big one. It is taken care of now, but it may involve several million dollars."
I thought that he was kidding because Danny always had a sense of humor, of some sort. I said to him, "Danny, don't kid me." He said, "Dad, I'm not kidding," and he began to explain what had happened.

He told me that a customer named Daryl Zimmerman, whom I wouldn't recognize if he walked into my office, had gone on the floor of the Exchange and traded several thousand U.S. 30-year bonds, going short. At the same time, an associate of his, trading thru Goldenberg, Hehmeyer, had been trading opposite in the bond options. This was a major disaster! I asked Danny, "What's happened?" because I didn't believe it and added,

*(L-R), Celebrating our years at the Board of Trade—
Frank Jost (50 years), Al Nelson (60 years), and the
youngster (40 years), 1990.*

"Who was it?" I thought that maybe it was an older, major customer of ours, who was involved and someone who may have "flipped his lid." But, no, it was Daryl Zimmerman who had been at the center of the scandal.

Danny explained to me that he had gone down to the Exchange floor and talked to officials about the situation without speculating on the error. So, along with one of my local customers, John Fyfe, who happened to be in charge of one of the major bond houses on the floor, they helped to liquidate the trades that had been made by Zimmerman. There were thousands of contracts of bonds sold short that had to be covered. That was accomplished, and, at the same time, Danny used the options market to help liquidate the problem. Meanwhile, upstairs, Jeffrey was working the computers to get the numbers together in order to assist in the liquidation.

When I arrived at our house in Florida, I called the CBOT Clearing Corporation and was told that we had to come up with $5 million immediately. There I was in Florida but immediately decided to return to Chicago on the next plane that afternoon. Still, I was told on the phone that they needed a commitment right then. I asked, "How much is the loss?" but they had no idea about the total... it could have been $20 million or $4 million. My response was, "I'll meet with you as soon as I get back. We need to find out what happened since we are the victims of illegal activities." They said, "No, we have to have a commitment from you right now! We talked to your bank, and they told us that they would back up anything you need."

Well, I hadn't talked to the bank, but later I discovered that the statement about the bank was not accurate. I said to them, "I'll meet you tomorrow morning, and let's go over this!" By the time we had the meeting, my company and I had already been threatened with expulsion by the clearing corporation even though nobody had any idea how much money was involved and who were the illegal participants. I soon learned that the FBI and the police had been called into the case.

Eventually I met with Billy O'Connor, chairman of the Board of Trade, Tom Donovan, president of the Board, Board attorneys, and people from the Clearing Corporation. I was informed that Lee B. Stern and Company was suspended, including my son Danny, Les Mouscher, and myself because our memberships were being held as collateral for any losses. Meanwhile, my company, which had assets that included our stock worth over $10 million, was suspended from trading. I asked the people at the meeting, "Why are we suspended?" Their response was that they were protecting the price of the memberships as part of our collateral. I asked, "What if I give you a check in the amount of all three memberships? Inasmuch as we are the victims, and if I put up that money, then there is no reason to hold our memberships." And, with that, Billy O'Connor said, "Lee, that's great. It's a terrific idea and I accept your solution because it is absolutely correct."

It looked like everything was going to be all right until the attorney for the Board of Trade told Billy that he still needed to check with his executive committee on the matter. Billy said, "I don't need to check with anyone," but the attorney insisted that Billy discuss my proposed solution with his committee. When he did talk to the committee, he was told that my solution was not acceptable. Tears were coming out of Billy O'Connor's eyes and I was absolutely incensed because a press release had already been written and sent out explaining the expulsion even though Billy said that he hadn't signed anything at that time. While Tom Donovan claimed that there wasn't a press release but just comments being made, Jeffrey phoned me to report that the story was all over the newspapers, radio, and television about the expulsion. As a result, Tom and I got into quite a heated argument. Fortunately there were no fists thrown, but I was very upset with how they were handling the situation.

On the following Monday, we discovered that we had incurred a loss of almost $8.5 million and I took steps to cover that loss. It took exactly two days, and my word, to make sure that the loss was taken care of in the Clearing Corporation. Needless to say, I felt pretty low even though we weren't broke, but we certainly weren't as financially secure as we had been prior to the event. A day or two later, I got a call from Jack Sandner, chairman of the Mercantile Exchange, of which I was a member. We had resigned our clearing privileges at the Merc that same day with no problem and no suspension at the Exchange. He invited me over to the semi-annual meeting they were having there, and I said that I just didn't feel up to attending to the meeting.

The Merc was giving out medals to its 25-year members, of which I was one. Instead, at the insistence of my family, including Jeffrey, Danny, Kenny, and January, I was encouraged to go and went over there despite still feeling down in the dumps. As I was sitting there and they were introducing different people to come up to receive their medals, they announced my name. As I got up to receive my recognition award, everybody in the room stood up, including all the executives and officers from the Merc, like Leo Melamed and Jack Sandner, and they applauded for me. I started to cry, and they hugged me. Everybody said that I had done the right thing by putting up the money when it was necessary, and they were proud of me. I will never forget that day and the way that the people at the Mercantile Exchange, where I was not active, handled the event. I only wish that some of the people at the Board of Trade had handled it that well. Certainly, Billy O'Connor couldn't have been better to me, but there were a few other people at the Board who didn't really seem to mind the fact that there had been a problem even though I was able to handle that problem.

The crisis made the headlines as well as costing my firm several million dollars because trades made were guaranteed by my firm even though the two individuals involved were trading illegally. Zimmerman and his associate were eventually sentenced to 41 months in Federal prison because of their activities. I stopped clearing after that because I didn't want to invest any more money in my company as a clearing firm, and I felt that the Board of Trade had not corrected the problem that had caused this in the first place. Indirectly, they never changed their rules, which could have prevented another similar crisis. There were other rule violations made by floor brokers, but they never suffered the consequences they should have experienced. In the end, I was awarded $8.5 million by the Board of Trade Arbitration Panel for which there was approximately $1.5 million to $2 million available. The suspensions of Danny, Lester Mouscher, and me were officially rescinded, which meant that those actions never occurred. My wallet was thinner but the Sterns' reputation remained intact.

This was probably the most difficult time I ever had during my career at the Board of Trade. But, even during this horrendous disaster, it was wonderful the way in which my close friends at both exchanges handled the situation. If you read about it in the newspapers the first day, or watched television, you would have difficulty separating the real victim from the criminals. But, thanks to the help of Irv Kupcinet and Terri Savage, whose advice I followed, as well as Dan Edelman, of Edelman and Associates, whom I hired to help with public relations, the real story was told, and by the following Monday, everyone knew who was the victim of the scam. The correct story was in the *Wall Street Journal*, the *New York Times*, and in *Barrons,* as well as all of the other important financial publications. But, that first day, the headlines reported that Stern and Company had been in a bond scandal, and that simply wasn't the case. As a demonstration of how the media can screw things up, they reported that the people involved in the scam were all employees of mine. Well, they weren't my employees at all! Zimmerman, who had an account with my firm, and his associate, Catalfo, who had an account with Goldenberg Haymeyer, were both CBOT members.

I really was indebted to Irv Kupcinet, who called me and wanted to know what had happened. When I told him, he urged me to contact Dan Edelman immediately for public relations advice. I did call Edelman, and we scheduled a meeting for the following Monday. Then, I heard from Terri Savage, whom I knew personally because I had appeared on her radio show several times, and who had also heard about the fiasco. She suggested that I not wait until Monday for my meeting with Edelman. Two days after the horrific event, Danny, Jeffrey, Kenny, and I met with Edelman in his apartment on Sunday morning. He told us what he intended to do, and I hired him. I also went on television with Walter Jacobson, who was known as a pretty tough interviewer. I had met Walter before, and he called me up because he wanted to get the story directly from me. My advice from Dan Edelman was not to do it because he thought that Walter would give me a rough time. I didn't think so, and I decided to go on television with Walter. I was very confident that Walter would treat me fair. I was right in my decision because he was terrific, and by the end of the interview, tears were flowing from both of us.

At the Board of Trade, there were political battles along the way including friends of mine with whom I disagreed. But they always knew my position on issues. As I look back, I realize that I was no shrinking violet in the pits, but part of it was that I was young at the time. I quickly learned that nobody was handing me anything and that I had to be tough in order to survive. The interesting part of being a member of the Board of Trade as well as a floor trader was that all I needed in my early years there was a card, a pencil, and a few dollars, and I do mean a few dollars. I know that in my first few years there I probably

Please join us in celebrating

Lee B's

60th Anniversary

as a member of

The Chicago Board of Trade

Wednesday, November 11, 2009

1:45 p.m.

The Standard Club

320 South Plymouth Court

Chicago

Hosted by:

Jeffrey, Danny, January and Kenny

R.S.V.P. Patti
312-461-8202

Lunch will be served

made some enemies as well as friends, but I never held a grudge. I had some terrific mentors, including John McCarthy, Herman Gordon, Stubby Sachs, and Milton Kirschbaum. But, from the standpoint of trading, I would say that it came natural to me.

Twice I was a director of the Board of Trade. I first ran for director in my 30s when I was a young guy. I was nominated for a directorship, but I was soundly beaten. I was probably a little too young and a little too aggressive for some people. Then, I ran again and was elected. Later I was appointed by Fred Uhlman for another term to fill a vacancy.

Stress was the rule when you traded at the Board, and one had to be able to stand the pressure. But, working there didn't seem to stress me. In fact, I didn't even notice it because it was an everyday part of the job. However, one needed to have the personality to do it, and couldn't be a wallflower or afraid to make quick decisions. The toughest part of being a trader is taking losses and knowing when to lose. I asked a very dear friend of mine, who is one of the biggest traders at the Exchange to this day, and who can be on the golf course and have huge positions, "What's the toughest decision you have to make?" His answer was, "The toughest decision is when to take profits. Taking losses is something I know how to do, because I am aware when I am going to take a loss. No matter what I think of the market, the key decision is how far you let the profits ride."

These comments came from Richard Stark, a longtime member and former director of the Chicago Board of Trade, and the most loyal customer and friend one could have. Richard's reputation as an outstanding speculator, businessman, and golfer extraordinaire, is a story in itself, and his reputation is impeccable.

I have always been able to do the loss part, but I have never been able to just let things ride. In the stock market, there are different methods used to make decisions, such as when a stock gets to a valuation that is 50 times earnings and it is clearly time to get out and let someone else get the profits. The same approach doesn't apply to the commodities market. That is true even more so today because now you have different problems, while it used to be just the issue of supply and demand that determined prices. Today, you have excess money that is following certain computer parameters that have no relationship to those factors.

My sons are independent traders, and they make their own decisions. Danny and Jeff are involved in the company on a daily basis and help to make policy decisions. Al Goldberg, a CPA, came to work for me around 1975 after being a partner in a public accounting firm and doing our company audit. I had just started a clearing company and needed someone with his experience. The timing couldn't have been better because it was a point when our business was exploding. Al fit in quite well, and he has been a very loyal member of my company, and a good friend. I may tease him a lot, and I certainly can be tough on him, but although we sometimes disagree, overall, we get along great.

I am also fortunate to have Mark Kirschner, another long time assistant as part of the company family. In addition, Marvin Parsoff, who retired two years ago, was an important part of our organization. As vice president, he was responsible for bringing the silver futures contract to the Chicago Board of Trade in the early 1970s. Our company was the

*((L-R), "The kid" with his only nephew,
Keith Bronstein. To think that he's a Cub fan.
How disappointing, but there's still hope!*

I was just looking for an approach to business in a different way, so I joined with a couple of guys and we started our own firm where I still am today. I can tell you that one of the many things I did learn from Lee was that there was no point in having any regret. I think that one of Lee's qualities and something he exemplified was that he trusted his instincts in business, and they have always been extraordinarily good. Some traders are very instinctive and you can't teach anyone that because it is either something you have or you don't. His instincts have been so good that he has been able to apply them to financial investments and to building his wonderful collection of fine art. He also applies those instincts to his selection of friends, and Lee is a very charitable person which includes both giving financially and of himself. All the things that he would organize and sponsor are amazing, and he did all of that despite a busy life, a family to watch over, and a career to build.

Charlie Carey

Lee Stern was known to many people as a colorful, flamboyant, and almost legendary figure at the Chicago Board of Trade and had been a contemporary of my father. When I started at the Board in 1978, when Lee came into the pits, he did his own trades. Depending on when you ran into him there, it could be a good day or a bad day, but he was always outspoken, never shy, and always a very aggressive, respected pit trader. Lee likes to mix it up, and he is not afraid to get into disagreements with people, so he has his good days and bad days. On those days when everything is going right, he is sociable and pleasant, while on his bad days he can be abrasive and argumentative.

Although I didn't really get to know Lee that well in my early years at the Board, despite being friendly, our relationship really grew when I became chairman of the Board of Trade. He was a great supporter and a great activist because we agreed on the direction of the Exchange. I would suggest that Lee has mellowed ever so slightly in his later years, but he can still be cantankerous and lively and animated and all of those things that describe Lee Stern.

Chapter 5
Sportsman: The Sting and The White Sox

blowing kisses to the fans, and Pato Margetic, with his long hair. And, nobody was more colorful than Willy Roy.

Today, my guess is that if you think about baseball and hockey players, over 50% of them are not American born and come from many different nationalities. Then there are the soccer-style kickers in professional football who were all foreign-based, and there are many foreign born players in professional basketball. So, now, nobody pays attention to the issue, but, in those days, it was a big negative for soccer, although we had the best bunch of American players in the NASL. That was due to Willy Roy because he played them when he was my head coach. You had to play a certain number of them: three or four at all times. But, he would bring in somebody as a substitute. Willy is one of my favorite "love-hate" guys because we had what might be described as a love-hate relationship. . . but not really. I think that it was a matter of both of our tempers. We are close friends to this day.

One important thing I will say about sports, and the Sting, goes back to the parade that we had down LaSalle Street in 1981 after winning the NASL championship. I was asked what I thought about that event, and my answer was, "Anybody who ever thought they would lead a parade down LaSalle Street was either nuts, had an ego surpassing anybody in the world, or should be in an insane asylum somewhere. Why would anybody think that they would ever lead a parade down LaSalle Street?" I think that if Willy Roy had another year of experience we would have probably won the championship in 1980 as well as 1981. But, by the time we won it again in 1984, the League was reduced to nine teams. I must say that my son, Kenny, has been responsible for my major interest in soccer because he's the one who played the sport from around 6th grade onward. Jeffrey and Danny played football because they didn't have soccer at their schools when they were growing up. Today, Jeffrey is the national treasurer of the American Youth Soccer Organization (AYSO) and the liaison between the AYSO and the U.S. Soccer Federation.

Later on, when the Sting played indoors at the Chicago Stadium from 1980-1986, I became friendly with Bill Wirtz. The Sting had some great sell-out crowds and Bill was a wonderful landlord to me with just a handshake deal. One day, Phil Woosnam, the NASL commissioner, requested a copy of our lease. Bill said he would have one for me to give to the league. A few days later, he called me and said his dad, Arthur, wanted to meet with me. He felt the Sting wasn't paying enough rent. Bill said, "Just see dad and say yes to any request." You and I have a deal, and that deal stands. Arthur Wirtz and I never met later, as he passed away before our meeting.

My only time that I recall meeting Arthur was at an indoor game when we first played at the Chicago Stadium. I asked him how he liked indoor soccer, and his reply stunned me. He said, "I like it better than hockey. I can see the damn ball."

I will always remember the enthusiastic support given to the Sting and Chicago soccer by five Chicago mayors: Mayor Richard J. Daley, Mayor Michael Bilandic, Mayor Jane Byrne, Mayor Harold Washington, and Mayor Richard M. Daley. In addition, we received continual encouragement and support from Governor James R. Thompson and Governor George Ryan.

Dutch International's Peter Ressel, also a popular Sting player at Wrigley Field, 1979.

Sting co-captain and midfielder, Ingo Peter in action at Cominsky Park, 1981

Of course I am forever indebted to Mayor Byrne for honoring the Sting when they won the NASL championship, and she hosted a wonderful parade down LaSalle Street and then to Michigan Avenue, along with a luncheon for 300 VIPs under a tent at Water Tower Place.

The Sting brought much happiness to the older generation of Chicagoans. When my mother was in her late 70s and early 80s, she went to all the Sting games, and my father-in-law, who was born in Russia, also attended all the Sting games. My private secretary, Ann Tully, who was also Dan Rice's secretary for a number of years, went to games with my mother. All of the older, foreign-born residents of Chicago used to come to the Sting games. So, what a thrill the team gave to that generation, and when we won the NASL championship in 1981, it was the first championship for a Chicago sports franchise since the Bears had won the NFL title in 1963. Soccer has become an American sport today. I was the only owner of the Chicago Sting, despite the fact that every once in a while I see the phrase "former owner of the Chicago Sting."

During the last year of the Sting's existence, I made a tremendous mistake. I gave an opportunity to a fellow named Lou Weisbach of Halo Advertising to buy into the team. He was in charge of all the marketing and front office. Unfortunately, for me and the Sting, and to the best of my memory, he never sold one marketing package or a season ticket. He owed me over $1 million as his part of the deal, but I settled with him for half that amount to get him out of my hair for good.

The FIFA Soccer World Cup has been an important part of my life dating back to 1986. Thanks to Clive Toye, I was introduced to Drummond Challis, a well known British sports director and producer. Lo and behold, I became the executive producer of *Hero*, the 1986 World Cup official film. Michael Caine narrated the movie for a fee of $10,000, but I think that as a soccer fan he would have probably been happy to pay us the $10,000 just to narrate the film.

Mexico City had suffered a tremendous earthquake a few months prior to the start of the World Cup, but they still managed to put together what is recognized as one of the most exciting events in World Cup history! *Hero* won several awards thanks to Drummond's remarkable work.

After the Sting closed its doors in 1988, my interest in soccer was confined to the U.S. National Team and the World Cup in 1990. I was honored by the U.S. Soccer Federation at a dinner in Chicago along with Dr. Henry Kissinger. Norma and I followed the team to Italy where we attended the World Cup. This particular event became famous for something other than soccer. Prior to the finals on July 7, 1990, the Three Tenors (Placido Domingo, Jose Carreras and Luciano Pavarotti) put together a charity concert which was held at the ancient Baths of Caracella in Rome. The site held 8,000 people, the weather was perfect, and the concert was spectacular. Norma and I agree that it was the most wonderful evening which we have ever experienced.

In 1994, the Three Tenors again appeared at the World Cup in Los Angeles at Dodger Stadium. For Norma and me it lacked the excitement of the first concert in Italy, but it was

(L-R), Sting Co-Captains Derek Spaulding and Ingo Peter holding the 1981 North American Soccer League Championship trophy as they get ready for the big parade in Chicago.

Pato Margetic, MVP, at the 1984 championship victory over the Toronto Blizzard.

also a very nice evening. Finally, in 1998, we attended the last of the World Cup concerts. It was held next to the Eiffel Tower in Paris, and needless to say, it was another wonderful occasion. Thanks to Alan Rothenburg, president of the U.S. Soccer Federation, and Hank Steinbrecher, secretary general of the Federation, we had front row seats at both events.

In 1998, with the Major Soccer League in its third year, Sunil Gulati, who is now president of the U.S. Soccer Federation, approached me about buying the Chicago franchise. The price tag was $5 million, a long way from the $250,000 cost for the NASL Sting franchise. I felt honored to have been asked, but after thinking it over and checking my bank account, I turned down the opportunity. Incidentally, the going price for the franchise, as I write this book, is $30 million!

However, my interest in the new league took on a new chapter in my life. Phillip Anschutz, owner of the Chicago Fire, and a Denver entrepreneur, purchased the Chicago franchise. I contacted him and offered my assistance as needed and I recommended Peter Wilt as a potential general manager. After several interviews with other prospects, Phil named Peter as the new boss of the Fire. I will always remember their first press conference because Phil said to the media, "Stern and the Sting set the plate, and we are going to put the food on it!" (or words to that effect). While I had no official role with the Fire, I always felt part of the organization thanks to Phil.

When the Fire won the Open Cup Championship on Frankie Klopas' golden goal, and later the MLS Championship, it was a great personal thrill for me! I felt that the Sting was still alive and well, thanks to the Chicago Fire and its class act on and off the field. When Commissioner Doug Logan gave me an Open Cup Championship medal, I was overwhelmed. Later, Mr. Anschutz sold the team to Andrew Hauptman and Andell Holdings. I wish Andrew well and continue to do so. It is great to know that Frank Klopas, a former Sting star, and one of the U.S. National team's star veteran soccer players is the Fire's technical director. I will always be grateful to Bob Bradley, the Fire's first coach and presently the U.S. National Team coach, for making me feel a part of the team.

Finally, in 2003, I was inducted into the National Soccer Hall of Fame along with many of my NASL colleagues. It was a fun evening, and I enjoyed a reunion with so many of the people responsible for the success of soccer in the United States today.

The White Sox

As for my role with the White Sox, it happened just after I had bought the Sting. Aaron Cushman, who had a major public relations company and was friendly with Bill Veeck, came to me and said, "Would you be interested in investing with Bill Veeck in the White Sox?" Don't forget that I was a Cub fan all my life, but I wasn't anti-Sox. Veeck needed money because Major League Baseball wouldn't let him own a team due to a certain level of required financing. I said, "Sure, I would be interested in exploring an investment." This came up in late 1975 which was my first year owning the Sting. I gave the offer some thought and decided that here I am just starting a soccer team, and nobody really knew

Sting players celebrating after winning the 1984 North American Soccer League Championship versus the Toronto Blizzard.

Karl Heinz-Granitza, the Sting's big star and leading scorer.

Sting in its early days, playing at Soldier Field c. 1976.

me. So, I figured that the investment could give me a broader entrée into sports owner-ship. I put together a group that included three other guys from the Board of Trade: the late Freddie Brzozowski; Harvey Yannick; and, Richard Dennis. We were the ones who kept the Sox in Chicago because we put together enough money to allow Bill Veeck to keep the team here and, as a result, our Board of Trade group owned about 20% of the team. I invested approximately $300,000 of my own money and, today, I have a 1.96% ownership of the team under the Reinsdorf banner.

My role today on the board of directors is not to just say "yes" to Jerry Reinsdorf, who serves as the managing partner. I say "no" a lot of times, but he doesn't often listen to me. I wonder why? When Veeck took over the team, we did have an executive committee, and I was on that committee. It is too bad that Bill wasn't as good managing money as he was at promotions. Then, as time went by, Veeck wanted to sell the team to Edward DeBartolo, who also owned an NFL team. The deal was almost completed, the team was going to be sold to DeBartolo, and Veeck got DeBartolo to guarantee all losses. On that issue, Veeck did a great job getting into DeBartolo's wallet. The word came back that it didn't look like DeBartolo was going to be allowed in by the League as an owner because of his racetrack connections, despite the fact that George Steinbrenner, the owner of the New York Yankees, also had racetrack connections. I don't think that the real reason for his being rejected by the League was ever publicized because DeBartolo never did sue anybody over the situation.

I received a phone call from Jerry Reinsdorf, whom I didn't know at the time, but who was recommended to me by a mutual friend. Yes, we have mutual friends! He asked me to meet him for lunch to get some information about the White Sox. So, we met at Orlando's restaurant located near the Board of Trade and owned by my best friend, George Assimos, who picked up the tab. When we sat down, Reinsdorf wanted to know why the bid he had submitted hadn't been selected. I said, "Jerry, I think that the real reason was that we had a single guy who could write a check and you are putting together a group of people who will need to get the money together. However, I don't think that DeBartolo is going to be able to close the deal. So, be patient, things may fall your way." And, sure enough, DeBartolo was turned down. Jerry ended up with a successful bid for $18 million for the team. Later on, I asked him, "Since you were the only bidder, why did you keep the bid at $18 million instead of lowering the offer?" His answer to me was, "Lee, once I made a bid, I made a bid!" That's the way that Jerry does business and he wasn't going to try to maneuver the offer backward. He felt that $18 million was a fair price and if he started playing around he might lose the deal.

There are about 12-13 members of the corporate general partnership, of which I am one. Jerry is the managing partner, and he now controls, in stock, the corporate general partnership. He asked me if I wanted to remain on the board of directors, and I agreed. One of the owners of the Chicago Bulls, Richard Stern (no relation), came to me to talk about an opportunity he faced years ago to invest in the Bulls. He asked me about Reinsdorf, and my response was, "You can go to the bank with whatever he tells you." He responded with, "That's good enough for me." He wound up with an interest in the Bulls now probably worth $30 million, and I ended up not joining the Bulls deal. So, today my financial interest in the Bulls is the cost of a season ticket and a free hot dog during Jerry's halftime feeding frenzy!

From my own standpoint, the issue was that I was not a basketball fan, but I was a 10% partner in Sportsvision. We owed $11.5 million, and my part of that was 10% with what looked like a losing situation. I felt like I was in good company. However, in order to stay involved in what may become a successful operation, I had to have a soccer team, the Chicago Sting. I kept that alive and it was burning a hole in my pocket.

Along with the Sting ownership as well as my investment in the White Sox, which was returning zero, I wasn't a basketball fan. I said to Jerry, "Why do you think that the Bulls are going to be successful?" He said, "For two reasons: pro basketball has never been promoted properly in Chicago (this was before anyone knew about Michael Jordan); and, secondly, the salary cap." We don't have a salary cap in baseball, but, in basketball, I think that it was 48% of the gross in those days. We shook hands, I wished him good luck, and didn't join the deal. I think that one point would have cost me $500,000. Could I have afforded it? Yes, and I could have had a partner like Henry Shatkin, who had been interested in the Bulls. But, the trouble was that I wasn't a basketball fan. I just didn't see the bigger picture at that time, and, besides, the Sting was outdrawing the Bulls indoors at the Chicago Stadium.

In 1983, soccer was very popular and we were drawing 15,000+ at the Stadium for indoor soccer. A year later, I saw Reinsdorf and I said to him, "You want to know something. If you were a good guy, you would let me into that Bulls deal." He answered, "I am not a good guy!" So, would my life have changed at all? Probably, not! My guess is that an investment of $500,000 at that time is now probably worth $30 million today and I may be low in my estimate. The question is: Do I regret it? The answer is, "sometimes yes and sometimes no. But, I don't think it would have changed my life except, perhaps, the Sting would still be alive in the MLS."

In terms of my role with the White Sox, there are several board of directors meetings in which we get a rundown on what is happening and discuss and vote on various financial matters. I would say that I speak to Jerry maybe once every couple of weeks. I talk to him about the overall business situation of the White Sox and baseball stuff, but my specific role is to drive him nuts. Jerry is very good at hiring people to make decisions about the day-to-day operations of the White Sox, and his staff, headed by Executive Vice President, and right-hand-man Howard Pizer, has been with him a long, long time. As for people who think that the owners are getting all these big, fat dividends, I can truthfully and honestly say that I can only remember one dividend that we got as part of profits. I think that the only real financial benefit will happen for the investors when the team is sold. The owners originally paid $18 million for the White Sox, and, today the team is

Lee and Norma at World Cup in Germany, 2006.
What a great time!!

What a thrill being part of the 2005 Chicago White Sox World Series Championship parade, north down LaSalle Street from the Board of Trade!

THOMAS #35
MAYOR RICHARD M. DALEY
GUILLEN
JERRY REINSDORF
KONERKO #14

CHICAGO DOUBLE DECKER CO.

773 648 5000
www.chicagodoubledecker.com

worth well over $500 million. But, I don't think that the team will ever be sold as long as Jerry is alive. As for me, it has been a great investment for my children and grandchildren and a lot of fun for Norma and myself.

While the Sting victory parade in 1981 was a fantastic experience for me, the 2005 White Sox World Series victory parade was unbelievable. The entire city was celebrating the first World Series championship since 1908, and the parade, which included all the players along with Ozzie, Kenny, and Jerry riding in open air buses, coaches, other owners, and Mayor Daley, proceeded from Cellular Field through all the South and West Side neighborhoods. I was in a bus with several White Sox players when we reached LaSalle Street and the Board of Trade. My memory of the Sting parade from 14 years earlier returned, but the enormous crowds that reached from State Street west to LaSalle could not be believed. It had to be the biggest parade reception in Chicago history even surpassing the astronauts and the Bulls, and it was certainly well deserved.

Incidentally, while Jerry is not a soccer fan, he did like indoor soccer, and he, and Eddie Einhorn, came to several Sting games at Chicago Stadium. However, Jerry stopped coming to the games when he accidentally stabbed himself while cutting a 50 lb. piece of a World's Famous Chocolate bar that was given to me in honor of my birthday during the Sting game. Not only did he get a piece of chocolate, which he later devoured, but Jerry suffered a major wound in his thigh. I had to take him to the team locker room so our team doctor could sew up his injury. Jerry's son, Michael, had warned his dad not to mess with the knife, but Jerry did not heed his advice. Michael, who was 13 years old at the time, has never let him forget it. This event, however, did not stop Eddie from attending further Sting games, indoors and out. Eddie, Jerry's original partner in the White Sox, is still listed as vice chairman, but he is not involved in the operational aspects of the team as he was in the past. I am glad that I had the opportunity of watching him in the world of sports. Eddie now resides in New Jersey.

*A real surprise from the Board of Trade
at the beginning of the 1981 victory parade.
Thats Norma Stern on Lee's right.*

My favorite photo showing Pele, on left, meeting
Chicago Bear founder, George Halas,on right at Soldier Field, 1976.

Sting Coach Willy Roy, 1981

team wins, you get all these extra awards that go along with it.

After 1981, we started to play indoor soccer as well and we also made it to the indoor championship. The games were played at the old Chicago Stadium, which was really a phenomenal place to play as well as having acoustics that were absolutely awesome. We relied on the same stars we had brought to Chicago for outdoor soccer, and I was lucky enough to have, without question, the best group of American players in the league. However, after that indoor season, we suffered a series of major injuries when we lost Arno Steffenhagen, who had anterior cruciate ligament damage, Pato Margetic, a young superstar whom we got from Detroit, who got injured, and Karl-Heinz Granitza, whose ankles were totally shot. We began the next outdoor season with a losing streak, but when our stars began to return from their injuries, the team started to show its old pizzazz again. In 1982, we ended up winning the Transatlantic Cup, by beating the Cosmos, Nacional from Uruguay, who were the World Club soccer champions at that time, and Napoli, from Italy. So, we were going in the right direction again.

In 1984, we won our second NASL title. However, after that year, the outdoor league folded and we began to play only indoor soccer. I believe that was an absolutely, total mistake. But, we were drawing well at the Chicago Stadium and the League decided to play a 40-game instead of a 24-game schedule. Stern recognized that this was a mistake and was the only negative vote. However, with the Blackhawks and the Bulls playing their home schedules at the Stadium, we didn't have a lot of good dates for our games. So, we were playing during the week when the kids were going to school and that hurt us since we were gearing everything to the younger generation to help develop an interest in soccer with new soccer fans. It meant that the whole thing kind of diminished, and I think that the worst part happened when we moved to the Rosemont Horizon (now the Allstate Arena) in Rosemont. That was simply not the same atmosphere as the Stadium and since the seating was not conducive to watching soccer it was as if we had moved to a minor league facility in comparison the old Chicago Stadium.

I stayed with the Sting until 1987. However, by that time, I think that Lee also lost a little enthusiasm, too, because he continues to tell me that he should have stopped with the 1984 season. In addition, we lost a lot of our good players and became just another team in the league. It reached a point where I couldn't sleep at nights because of the combination of stress, the years of coaching both indoor and outdoor soccer teams, as well as scouting and other responsibilities. After the team that year got off to a bad start with a record of 0-5, I met with Lee and he suggested to me that I should take some time off and drop my loyal and knowledgeable assistant coach, Mike Grbic. I wouldn't do that because when I was on scouting trips I never worried about the team with Grbic in charge. So, it came to a point where I went home and talked to my wife about the whole situation. I think that was the first night I had slept well in months. The next morning she said to me, "Willy, I think that it is time for you to go." I called Lee up and told him I was done as coach of the Sting.

Subject Index